DU

The Library of Physics™

THE LAWS OF MOTION
Understanding Uniform and Accelerated Motion

Betty Burnett, Ph.D.

The Rosen Publishing Group, Inc., New York

To Robert

Published in 2005 by The Rosen Publishing Group, Inc.
29 East 21st Street, New York, NY 10010

Library of Congress Cataloging-in-Publication Data

Burnett, Betty, 1940–
The laws of motion : understanding uniform and accelerated motion / Betty Burnett.
     p. cm. — (The library of physics)
Includes bibliographical references and index.
ISBN 1-4042-0335-4 (library binding)
1. Motion—Juvenile literature.
I. Title. II. Series: Library of physics (Rosen Publishing Group)
QC133.5.B87 2004
531'.11—dc22

                                                      2004011073

Manufactured in the United States of America

On the cover: An amusement park ride demonstrates circular motion

Contents

Introduction   4

1 Describing Motion   6

2 Mechanics and Motion   13

3 Newton's Laws of Motion   20

4 Forces That Act on Motion   30

5 Describing Motion with Graphs   40

Glossary   43

For More Information   44

For Further Reading   45

Bibliography   46

Index   47

Introduction

Speed is exciting to most people. Take, for instance, the many thrill seekers who participate in sports that depend on speed. Skateboarding, downhill skiing, basketball, cycling, and stock car racing are all fast and exciting. They are all about speed and motion. A good athlete must understand how to work with the laws of motion in order to be successful.

Drivers, pilots, and ship captains also use the laws of motion. They must know how to bank a turn, how to avoid a collision with another vehicle, and how to stop quickly and safely. Engineers and technicians use the laws of motion in designing products, from SUVs to guns, toys to space vehicles.

The laws of motion are a major part of the science of physics, the study of forces and matter. Classical physics (also called Newtonian physics) is concerned with the way in which matter responds to forces and the way in which forces act on matter. Everything that can be touched is made up of matter. Matter, in turn, is made up of atoms and molecules that move at the submicroscopic level.

Athletes like this downhill skier must understand the laws of motion, although they might not be conscious of the science behind the laws. Instead of studying the laws of physics, athletes usually learn through practice how factors such as direction, friction, and speed will affect their performance.

Since all matter is subject to forces, everything on the planet (living and nonliving) is subject to the laws of physics. These laws were not invented but were discovered through observation. Classical physics describes an ideal world through these laws. Some of the most basic laws in physics are about motion.

1 Describing Motion

otion is an action that occurs when something changes places or moves from point A to point B. Motion is constant around us. Even in a quiet spot in the country, leaves flutter in the wind or drop from their branches. A pebble may roll downhill when dislodged by an insect and birds take off in flight seeking air currents to ride. Cities are often a whirl of motion of never-ending traffic and machinery.

We can hardly imagine a motionless world. We are so used to working with motion that we can even distort it electronically with instant replays of sports events in slow motion or by fast-forwarding a DVD.

In studying motion and the forces that act on motion, the most important factors to determine are magnitude (size), direction, speed or velocity (the rate of movement), and displacement (the distance moved). Magnitude, direction, velocity, and displacement are expressed mathematically with numbers and formulas.

These mathematical quantities are divided into two categories: scalars and vectors. Scalars describe a magnitude only. Time and distance are scalars. For example, one hour and five miles are both scalar quantities.

Vectors describe both magnitude and direction. Direction is as important in the study of motion as magnitude is. Knowing that José's Video Store is eight miles away does not help anyone find it. The person in search of the store needs to know that it is eight miles north, south, east, or west of a certain landmark. It is necessary to know the direction an object has traveled to calculate its displacement, or how far it has traveled.

Speed is a measure of how fast an object is moving without regard to its direction. It is a scalar quantity. Speed is always measured in terms of time—how fast an object is going within a certain time frame—per hour, per minute, or per second.

Velocity measures the rate at which an object changes its position. It is a vector quantity because it concerns both magnitude and direction. A person jogging in place has zero velocity because he or she is not moving in a direction. The speed of a person jogging on a treadmill or using a stationary bicycle can be measured, but the velocity cannot. Velocity can be constant (uniform), or it can be accelerated.

A vector diagram is an illustration of an object while it is moving. It shows direction and magnitude.

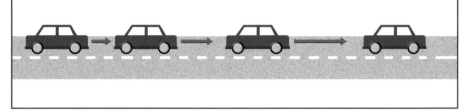

This vector diagram shows the velocity of a car in motion. The car is increasing its velocity, as shown by the lengthening arrows at each travel increment, which means it is accelerating. A vector diagram showing a car moving at a constant velocity, which is not accelerating, would have arrows of the same length at each increment of the car's motion.

How Fast Is Fast?
The Land Speed Record Accelerates

Since the invention of the gasoline engine, race car drivers have tried to set records for being the fastest in the world. The first land speed record set was for a car going 30 miles (63 kilometers) per hour. In less than 100 years, the record was pushed to over 700 miles (1,200 km) per hour, and today's drivers are wondering how to make it 1,000 miles (1,609 km) per hour.

1898 – 39.23 mph (63.13 km/h)
1904 – 91.37 mph (147.04 km/h)
1927 – 174.833 mph (281.447 km/h)
1935 – 301.129 mph (484.818 km/h)
1960 – 406.50 mph (654.359 km/h)
1965 – 576.553 (927.873. km/h)
1983 – 633 mph (1,018.7 km/h)
1997 – 763.035 mph (1,227.9 km/h)

Uniform Motion

When an object is maintaining a steady, unchanging speed, it is demonstrating uniform motion. Planets in orbit maintain uniform motion because the forces that keep them in motion are balanced. Therefore, astronomers can predict exactly where the planets will be on any given date. The hands of a clock are calibrated to move uniformly at the same speed so that they can measure time. In the real world, it is

The orbit of planets is a good example of uniform motion. Unless acted on by an outside force, every object will remain in the state it's in, whether it is at rest or in motion. Planets remain in motion, and the forces that act on them (namely gravity) cause them to move in predictable patterns.

very difficult to maintain uniform motion because of friction and gravity. Usually objects accelerate, or speed up or slow down.

Constant, or uniform, speed can be determined simply by dividing the distance covered by the time taken to travel that distance. The formula is $r = d / t$, or: the rate of speed is equal to distance traveled, divided by the time it takes to travel that distance. When the speedometer in a car reads 35 mph (56 km/h) it means that it takes one hour for a car at that speed to travel 35 miles (56 km). The distance, 35 miles (56 km), is divided by the time, one hour, to give a rate of 35 mph (56 km/h).

Acceleration

Acceleration changes motion so that it is no longer uniform. Acceleration is not the same as either speed or velocity. While speed measures the rate of motion, and velocity measures rate of motion and its direction, acceleration measures how quickly velocity changes. Acceleration is a vector quantity because it has both magnitude and direction. Acceleration includes slowing down as well as speeding up. An object with a constant (uniform) velocity is not accelerating because it is neither slowing down nor speeding up.

In order to calculate acceleration, the rate of change of motion, it is necessary to understand the vectors involved. The rate of change in the motion of an object depends on time, speed, and direction. An object at rest has zero motion, zero acceleration, and zero velocity or speed. When it begins to move, it accelerates. It will continue to move at a steady rate unless another force is applied to increase its velocity, decrease its velocity, or stop it.

A car driving at 35 mph (56 km/h) may change its speed to 50 mph (80 km/h) or to 20 mph (32 km/h). Either way, it is technically accelerating, although for clarity, we usually say that speeding up is accelerating and slowing down is decelerating.

Acceleration may be constant, that is, it may increase in definite units, from 1 to 2 to 3 to 4 for a period of time until the acceleration levels off or stops. The rate of acceleration may change second by second: faster, slower, faster, slower. Nothing on Earth can keep accelerating forever because acceleration is always limited by natural forces—gravity, friction, or tension.

Distance and Displacement

Distance is a scalar quantity. It is a measurement of how much ground a moving object covers during its motion. It is expressed in linear measurements— centimeters, inches, miles, kilometers, and so forth. Displacement is a vector quantity measuring how far the moving object has traveled from its origin. It describes the object's change in position from a point in space.

11

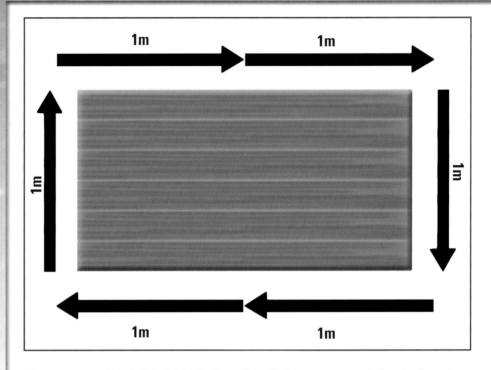

If a man standing behind his desk walks all the way around the desk and returns to where he started, how far has he gone? The two answers to this question reflect the difference between distance and displacement. The distance he has walked, which reflects motion, is 1 + 1 + 1 + 1 + 1 + 1, so we could say the man has traveled 6 meters. But we could also argue that he has gone nowhere, since he ended his journey precisely at the point from where he started. His displacement is 0 meters.

If a vehicle travels in a complete circle and stops, there is no displacement, even though there has been motion and distance traveled, because its end point is the same as its beginning point. The distance that it has traveled will be equal to the magnitude of the circle, which may be any number, depending on the circle's size.

2

Mechanics and Motion

The branch of physics concerned with motion is mechanics. Mechanics is usually thought of in connection with machines and how they work. In physics, mechanics refers to the motion of objects and the forces and energies that influence motion.

Mechanics is divided into two parts: kinematics and dynamics. Kinematics deals with how objects move, without regard to the cause of the motion. Objects may move in a straight line or take a circular path. Dynamics deals with forces and energy to explain why objects move as they do. The force behind a motion may be applied, such as steam, or it may be constant, such as the pull of gravity.

The Dimensions of Motion

Motion is dimensional because it takes up space (dimension) and requires time. The dimension of time (t) is always implied in motion because a change in location takes time to accomplish. Without time, there is no movement, just as there is no movement without direction.

Kinematics

The Greek root word *kine* means "motion." When motion pictures (movies) were first invented, they were also known as cinematics. "Cinematics" was shortened to "cinema," a familiar name for a movie theater. Kinetic art is sculpture that moves, such as mobiles (another word that means movement). Kinesics is the study of how non-verbal body motions such as shrugs, blushes, and smiles relate to overall communication.

The dimensions of motion are the direction that motion takes. In real life, motion has many dimensions because objects may go in many directions. One-dimensional (1-D) motion occurs only on paper. It traces a movement that goes back and forth along one axis (x). Two-dimensional (2-D) movement is back and forth (one dimension) and up and down. That is, it occurs on both x and y axes. Three-dimensional motion (3-D) adds a z axis, which may be interpreted as side-to-side motion. Three-dimensional motion may be imagined spatially from a diagram on paper. A wind-up toy may go from side to side, back and forth, and even somewhat up and down.

Determining the direction of motion is the first step in understanding the mechanics of motion. In a pinball game, movement seems to go in all directions at once, but if the motion is analyzed closely, it can be seen that each ball travels in a direct line from post to post. Each ball follows the basic form of motion, which is linear.

Linear Motion

Linear motion is movement in a straight line. Up, down, sideways, or diagonally, it doesn't matter which direction the object takes. As long as it stays in a straight line, it is traveling in a linear path.

A pinball, with its frenetic zigzagging motions, seems to move about in many different ways. But whatever the direction, the ball travels only linearly. Even when something gets in the ball's path and it is forced to move in a different direction, it is still moving only in a straight line.

All motion begins as linear. If a force prevents it from moving forward in a straight line, it angles off and takes another path, as the ball does when it hits a post in a pinball game, or a hockey puck does when hit by a stick. Any object that is heavier than air and is dropped or thrown to the ground falls downward in a linear motion.

Circular Motion

If an object is moving at a constant speed, but for some reason cannot move in a straight line, it will travel in a circle. That is, if its forward movement is limited and if it is not pulled back by mechanical means (as, for example, a paddle ball is), it will turn in an arc to keep moving.

Planets revolving around the Sun are examples of circular motion. They are prevented from continuing out into space in a straight line because gravity pulls them back toward the Sun. They are locked into their orbits by the force of gravity.

Centripetal force pulls any object in orbit toward the center of its orbit, the circle that it is moving in. There appears to be a force pulling it away from the center as well. This is called centrifugal force, but instead of being a real force, it is really the object's tendency toward linear motion, away from the center of a circle.

Children riding a playground merry-go-round experience this phenomenon. As the merry-go-round

This well-known amusement park ride uses forces involved with circular motion to make its riders laugh and scream. Riders stand at the wall of the circular machine, which begins to spin. As the machine gathers speed, riders are pinned against the wall by centrifugal force, and the floor drops out.

goes faster and faster, they feel pulled outward and have to hang on to keep from flying off their seats. By holding on to a bar, they apply centripetal force to counterbalance the centrifugal force, and that allows them to stay on.

Rotary Motion

If an object turns around an axis (a straight line or pole), it is demonstrating rotary motion. A bicycle wheel and a Ferris wheel are examples of rotary motion. They spin around an axis. All spinning objects, such as wheels, gyroscopes, and tops will continue to rotate in a circle until gravity or friction slows them down. Applied energy, such as electrical current, continues to add force to rotary motion and overcomes gravity and friction. Only when there is an imbalance in the system will the motion stop.

When a pitcher throws a baseball toward the opposing batter, the ball's trajectory is a projectile motion. As soon as the ball leaves the pitcher's hand, as shown in the above photo, it is acted on by the forces of gravity and is immediately drawn downward, so that its path forms an arc.

Projectile Motion

Projectile motion is a special case of motion. A projectile is an object propelled or expelled by force. Once it is expelled, the only force acting upon it is gravity. Projectiles travel in a trajectory, a curved path through space. They may be thrown or propelled vertically (upward or downward) or horizontally.

A thrown baseball or football is a projectile. Because of the pull of gravity, once the ball leaves the player's hand, it has a constant downward acceleration. This downward pull first slows the ball's original upward speed and then increases its downward speed as it falls back to earth. A baseball pitcher or quarterback learns how a thrown ball behaves under all conditions by trial and error and by feel, not by making mathematical models. An archer or sharpshooter must also learn the behavior of projectiles by feel. He or she has to learn to aim higher than the target, knowing that the arrow or bullet will lose some height due to gravity.

Ballistics is the science dealing with the motion of bullets. When fired from a gun, bullets become projectiles propelled through space by explosive energy. This burst of energy is strong enough to overcome gravity for a moment. The initial force carries the bullet forward until the pull of gravity drags it downward. A bullet by itself cannot do damage; throwing a bullet won't hurt anyone. It is the velocity of the bullet that allows it to injure or kill.

3

Newton's Laws of Motion

Isaac Newton (1642–1727) is considered one of the most important scientists of all time. Through studying gravity, he formulated laws of motion. Newton predicted the behavior of objects in different circumstances and then compared his predictions with what he observed in his experiments. He used his results to check his theories. In this way he created the scientific method.

Newton developed three laws to explain what he observed about motion when he determined that the same results always happen under the same circumstances. These three laws predict what will happen when an object starts to move or stops moving, and they explain why this happens. These laws are the basis of mechanics, the science of motion.

Newton's First Law of Motion

An object at rest tends to stay at rest and an object in motion tends to stay in motion with the same speed and in the same direction unless acted upon by another force. Or, any object not subject to outside

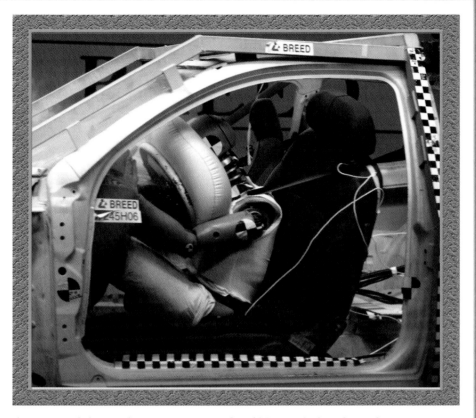

An automobile accident is one example of Newton's first law of motion at work. When a moving car stops suddenly, its passengers continue their forward projection until they are stopped by the obstruction of seat belts, a windshield, or as in this photo, an airbag. The force of that obstruction generally moves passengers backward, where they are stopped by the obstruction of their seat and headrest.

forces remains at a constant velocity (even if the velocity is zero) covering equal distances in equal times along a straight-line path.

Newton's first law is often called the law of inertia. It states that if an object is not being pushed or pulled by a force, it will either stay still or keep moving at a steady speed. The tendency of an object to remain moving or to remain motionless is called inertia. This notion of an object's tendency to resist acceleration is an important cornerstone of Newton's work. Before Newton, people thought that moving objects would eventually stop moving on their own. Newton proved that objects slow down, speed up, or stop moving only when a force outside themselves makes them.

Once an object is in motion, it tends to stay in motion unless something stops it. The resistance to slowing down is called momentum. Momentum is the tendency of an object to continue moving, whether it moves at a steady rate or accelerates. Momentum has both magnitude (size) and direction. It is a vector quantity.

The mathematical quantity for momentum (p) can be found by multiplying mass (m) times velocity (v).

$$p = m \times v$$

This measures the constant or unchanging movement of a moving object, whereas acceleration measures the changing rate of a moving object.

Momentum can be changed only by changing the object's velocity through acceleration or by changing its mass.

Similar to inertia is equilibrium, the state in which all forces are perfectly balanced. There is just as much pull as push. In a state of equilibrium, it takes the presence of a new force to trigger acceleration. This new force causes the balanced system to be unbalanced and brings about acceleration. Newton's second law explains this concept.

Newton's Second Law of Motion

The acceleration of an object as produced by a net force is directly proportional to the magnitude of the net force, in the same direction as the net force, and inversely proportional to the mass of the object. This can be represented mathematically by $a = \frac{F}{m}$, although the equation is normally written as $F = ma$.

This law sounds more complicated than it really is. It states that when a force acts on an object, the object accelerates in the direction the force is pushing or pulling it. If you push something forward, it goes forward.

And, the greater the object's mass, the more force is needed to make it move. It takes more force to

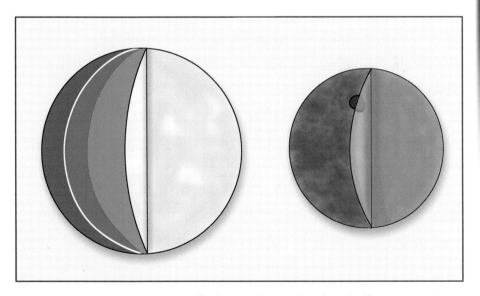

Although a beach ball is usually larger than a bowling ball, its mass is much less. This is because a beach ball is filled with air, which has very little weight, and a bowling ball is almost solid throughout. The bowling ball will move faster because of its mass, which also makes it more difficult to move it or change its direction.

move a semi than a sports car and more force to pull a Great Dane than a cocker spaniel puppy.

A proportional effect directly impacts the object. For instance, doubling the force that is used on an object will make the object accelerate twice as fast. A huge engine in a small car will make the car fly down a highway. An inverse proportional effect has an opposite impact on an object. If a constant force is applied, doubling the mass will make the object's acceleration one-half as large. For instance, a large truck needs more accelerating power than a smaller vehicle.

Newton's second law emphasizes the concept of mass. Mass is the amount of matter an object has. Every object has mass, but some objects are denser than others because their matter is more compact. Size is important in determining mass, but density is more important. Air is not very dense, but metal is, so a ball bearing has more mass than a balloon, although a balloon may be much larger.

The mass of a series of balls can be compared by hefting each one—a Ping-Pong ball, softball, basketball, bowling ball, and beach ball. Each has its own feel, its weight in relation to its size. Ever try to catch a bowling ball? The much larger beach ball is lighter and easier to catch because it has less mass and more air. But because it has less mass, it won't roll as well as the heavier bowling ball.

Mass influences the motion of an object. Given a constant force, the greater the object's mass, the slower it can change its velocity. An elephant cannot run as fast or change direction as quickly as a squirrel. Mass is significant not just because it describes how large and heavy an object is, but because it is the measure of an object's inertia. The more mass an object has, the more inertia it has. A box filled with bricks has more inertia than an equal-size box filled with Styrofoam, and it will take more force to move it. The box with less resistance to movement has less mass.

Newton's Third Law of Motion

The force that is exerted on one body by a second body is equal in magnitude and opposite in direction to the force exerted by the second body on the first. Or, if an object is pushed or pulled, it will push or pull to an equal extent in the opposite direction. This is often restated as, "For every action, there is an equal and opposite reaction."

Whenever object A and object B interact with each other, they exert forces upon one another. If a man pushes on a heavy van, he will feel the van push back on him. When a girl on ice skates pushes against the wall that runs along the rink, she will slide back on the ice. The direction of the force on the first object is opposite to the direction of the force on the second object.

If a bulldozer pushes against a wall in an attempt to demolish it, the wall will exert an equal and opposite force on the bulldozer. The bulldozer will destroy

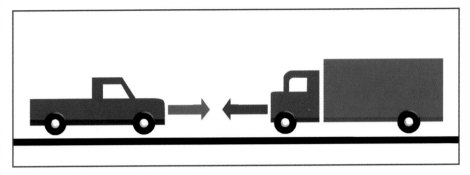

Common sense might tell you that when the two trucks shown above collide, the force on the smaller truck will be greater than the force on the larger truck. That is not the case, however. The collision exerts an equal force on each of the two trucks, according to Newton's third law.

the building only if it applies more force than the wall can withstand.

Someone trying to cross a lake in a rowboat must exert force against the waves to counteract the force that the waves exert against the boat. This example can be seen in thousands of everyday activities. Bicyclists, hikers, runners, weight lifters, and other athletes use the theory of opposing forces, although they may not be aware of it.

Conservation of Momentum

The law of conservation of momentum is an offshoot of Newton's third law and is a fundamental concept of classical physics. It states that the total momentum of all bodies in a closed system is constant and not affected by processes occurring within the system. The "processes occurring within the system" usually refers to a collision between objects.

The law of conservation of momentum is expressed mathematically as $mv_1 = mv_2$. The forces are equal in magnitude but they are opposite in direction. The total momentum of two objects before a collision is equal to the total momentum of the two objects after the collision. Nothing is added or subtracted; nothing changes. The total momentum of the objects before the collision is zero, since their directions are opposite. The total momentum after the collision is zero because they are not moving.

Momentum cannot be lost, but it can be transferred from one object to another. When a pitcher throws a baseball, the catcher catches the momentum of the ball, as well as the ball itself.

A Clue About Cue Balls

The game of pool demonstrates the law of conservation of momentum. The object of the game is to make the cue ball collide with another ball so that the second ball will move in a specific direction. The collisions may be straight-on or off-center, and the skilled player will know exactly where and how to aim the cue ball to get the desired result. The momentum of the cue ball is transferred to the ball it hits, which gives it enough momentum to travel into a pocket. In a collision, the momentum lost by one object by its sudden stop is gained by the object it hits. The total amount of momentum remains constant. What object A loses is gained by object B.

When this moving eight ball collides with the stationary two ball, both balls experience forces of equal magnitude because they have the same mass. They will have equal accelerations (the moving eight ball will slow down and the standing two ball will speed up), and the eight ball will move back toward the direction from which it started.

Conservation of momentum occurs in the collision of a bat with a ball. When a batter hits a baseball, the momentum of the bat just before it strikes the ball plus the momentum of the pitched baseball is equal to the momentum of the bat after it strikes the ball plus the momentum of the hit baseball. The same is true in the collision of two automobiles or two football players.

As another example, imagine a boy balancing on a log. The total momentum of the boy and the log is zero because neither is moving. If the boy jumps off the log, he acquires forward momentum. At the same time the log moves in the other direction with an equal and opposite momentum. The total momentum of the boy plus the log remains at zero.

4

Forces That Act on Motion

A force is required to start, accelerate, stop, or redirect a motion. A force is not required to keep an object in motion; inertia does that. If no force acts upon an object at rest or in motion, it will continue to remain at rest or in motion. This is Newton's first law. If a force acts on an object at rest and there is no opposing force, it will accelerate in the direction of the force. This is Newton's second law.

Force exists when there is an interaction between two objects, that is, when one object pushes or pulls the other. This is Newton's third law. A tow truck applies force to pull a car that can't start; a tugboat applies force to push a barge into port. When the interaction stops, the objects no longer experience force. Some forces are not so obvious. Magnetic fields may attract or repel an object only slightly. Gravity is such a common pull that we are hardly aware of it.

Force is measured in newtons. One newton is the amount of force required to give a 1-kilogram mass an acceleration of 1 meter/second/second

($1m/s^2$). A newton is abbreviated as "N." Ten newtons of force is written as 10 N.

Types of Forces

Forces can be divided into two categories: forces that touch the object and forces that work from a distance and are not in contact with the object. Gravity and electromagnetism, for example, work from a distance. Friction and tension are two forces that work by contact.

Sir Isaac Newton (1642–1727) is one of the most influential scientists in history. Much of what we know about science today is based on the work he did about 300 years ago.

A roller coaster, for example, relies on both kinds of forces for movement and uses no engine to propel it. The cars of a roller coaster are usually pulled by a chain (friction) up to the top of the first hill, which is the highest. When the chain is released, the roller coaster races downhill. It relies on the energy in the force of gravity to move it once it gets going. Each hill after the first one is a little bit lower than the last one. Inertia keeps the

Many of the amusement park rides enjoyed by thrill seekers operate heavily on the laws of physics. A roller coaster is perhaps the best example, as it makes use of natural forces entirely. Instead of using an engine to propel the cars up to the peaks, down to the valleys, and around corkscrew turns, a roller coaster is designed to run on energy from natural forces such as friction and gravity.

roller coaster moving forward when the track is level or uphill.

Gravity

Gravity is the pull of one object toward the center of the mass of another. On Earth, we usually think of gravity as pulling downward. In space, the force of one body, such as Earth, the moon, or another massively large object, attracts other objects toward itself. The force gravity exerts on an object is exactly

Astronauts ride in NASA's KC-135 aircraft, more commonly known as the vomit comet. This training vessel allows riders to experience thirty-second sessions of weightlessness, making it invaluable for medical studies, motion-sickness experiments, gravity research, and preparation for space travel.

G Forces

Some acceleration g forces:

Event	Typical car	Sports car	F-1 Race car
starting	0.3–0.5	>0.9	1.7
braking	0.8–1.0	>1.3	2
cornering	0.6–1.0	>2.5	3

(Glenn Elert, "The Physics Hypertextbook," http://www.hypertextbook.com)

proportional to the object's mass. This means that the more massive (heavier and denser) an object is, the greater the pull of gravity will be.

"G force" measures acceleration due to gravity. The normal, earthbound "g" is 1. We can feel the results of anything less or more in our bodies. NASA (National Aeronautics and Space Administration) has studied the effects of weightlessness (0 g) for years and has developed ways to lessen its detrimental effects. Under natural conditions, there is no situation that involves long-term weightlessness on Earth. It is possible for a person to feel weightless for a second or two if he or she is thrown up into the air by mechanical means.

A moderate g force (less than 3) is exciting, as experienced on an amusement park ride or when an airplane takes off. A g force of 4 to 6 is too powerful for the average person to tolerate because it deprives the brain of blood flow. If such a g force lasts for more than half a minute, it can cause a fighter pilot to black out. To keep from losing consciousness, high-altitude pilots wear pressure suits that squeeze the torso, forcing blood to remain in their heads. People rarely survive anything higher than 8 g's for longer than a few seconds.

Friction

The most common force that causes objects to slow down (accelerate in a negative direction) is friction.

Skydivers count on their parachutes to counter the force of gravity that pulls them downward. The friction of the open chute causes skydivers to decelerate, slowing down their falls and softening their landings.

Friction acts like a drag on an object's speed. Friction is the force exerted by a surface as an object moves across it or makes an effort to move across it. It is a force applied in the opposite direction of an object's velocity.

All objects provide friction. Liquids, solids, and gases provide friction. The friction in sandpaper or an emery board quickly wears away a surface. Highways are built to provide the right amount of friction for tires. Too little friction (bald tires or icy conditions) can be hazardous because the car will not be able to stay on the road and will slide off. Friction is necessary for slowing or stopping a vehicle.

Air resistance is a frictional force that acts upon objects as they travel through air. It opposes the motion of the object. Skydivers and downhill skiers encounter air resistance. Race cars are designed to encounter as little air resistance as possible.

Objects traveling through water also meet resistance. A sailboat on a lake trying to get to a pier may be blown off course by air resistance and will then have to compensate for water resistance as well. Crew members have to use all their sailing skills to counterbalance these forces. In many cases, friction can be overcome by applying lubrication or smoothing a surface. One example is Teflon, a solid lubricant that is used to cut down on friction.

Applied Force, Normal Force, Spring Force, and Tensional Force

Applied force is a force applied to an object by a person or another object. It can either push or pull an object. If a person pushes a desk across the room, the person is applying force to the desk to make it move. An active force (such as when someone pushes a desk) is an applied force, unlike a passive force (gravity), which is simply present. When energy must be added to overcome inertia and gravity, it is applied through muscle or machine.

"Normal" force is the support force exerted upon an object in contact with another object. The contact between the two objects must be perpendicular—a lamp on a table, for instance, or a book on a shelf. If one object is resting on a surface, the surface is exerting an equal force against the object in order to support the object's weight.

A spring force is the force exerted by a compressed or stretched spring upon any object that is attached to it. An object that compresses or stretches a spring is always acted upon by a force that restores the object to the rest or equilibrium position. For most springs, the magnitude of the force is directly proportional to the amount of stretch or compression.

Tension is an oppositional force, that is, it is created when forces act at opposition to each other.

Children have so much fun hopping around on pogo sticks that they don't even realize that a fundamental force of physics is at work. The force of the rider's weight compresses the spring at the bottom of the pogo stick and as the spring restores its shape, it exerts a force equal to the force of its compression, propelling the rider into the air.

For example, when a wire is pulled tight, tension is transmitted through it because forces act from each end. The tensional force is directed along the wire and pulls equally on the objects on either end of the wire.

Objects that are being pulled or pushed may create a dynamic system, one that produces change. Energy is always present in a dynamic system, and energy is often represented by a force. This representation, however, is incorrect. Technically, energy is a scalar quantity; force is a vector quantity. Forces may be opposed or unopposed. An opposing force will counter-act another force. For instance, the force of a rocket taking off can counteract the force of gravity.

Usually, many forces, not just one, work on objects. One force may be influenced by the presence of another one—magnetic, gravitational, and electric forces often work together.

5 Describing Motion with Graphs

The language that describes motion is mainly mathematical and uses equations to define various terms. While these equations and the math involved can be confusing to people who are used to a literary or ordinary language, it does help make mathematics universally understandable. The information used to explain motion in mathematical language can also be "translated" into graphs and diagrams, which are easier for some people to understand.

Free-Body Diagrams

Free-body diagrams are a form of mathematical language. They are used to show the relative magnitude and direction of all forces acting upon an object in a given situation.

To make a free-body diagram, choose an object that is subject to motion—a car, a bullet, a person, or anything that can move or be moved. Give this object a shape. In the diagrams below, the object is represented by a square, but it could be a more realistic representation. Show all the forces that are acting on this object with arrows. This diagram can then be read.

Diagram 1 shows four forces acting on an object (the square): normal force, applied force, gravitational force, and friction. The size of the arrow represents the magnitude of the force. In this case the forces are equal in magnitude.

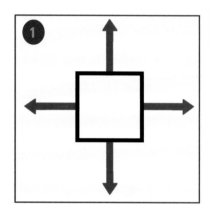

The direction of each arrow reveals the direction in which the force is acting.

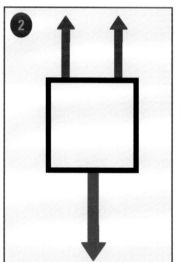

A child hangs from a trapeze suspended from the ceiling by two chains. Diagram 2 represents the tension force present in the chains and the gravitational force that is acting on the child.

A skydiver falls through the air at a constant velocity. Air resistance slows him down. Diagram 3 shows this situation.

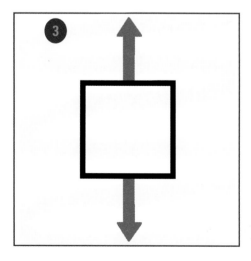

A car coasts to the right and slows down. Several forces are at work in this situation: normal, friction, and gravity. This free-body diagram shows them.

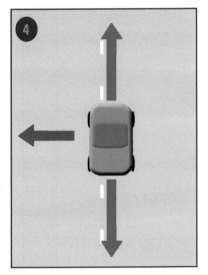

Graphs, charts, diagrams, and maps are helpful because they visually communicate complicated information. Once the basics are understood, they can be read quickly without the need to use words. Graphs and diagrams are used in newspapers and magazines around the world and need no translation. They demonstrate the essence of physical laws and illustrate the way things work.

We understand how machinery works because of Isaac Newton. Newton's three laws of motion laid the groundwork for modern physics. His understanding of mechanics paved the way for the Industrial Revolution and the hundreds of thousands of machines that have been invented over the past 300 years.

Glossary

acceleration (ak-sell-uh-RAY-shun) Any change in the velocity of an object.

displacement (dis-PLAYS-ment) The measure of how far an object has moved from its starting point.

force (FORS) A physical influence that moves something. ʂ.

friction (FRIK-shun) The force exerted by a surface as an object moves or attempts to move across it.

inertia (ih-NUR-sha) Resistance to change; the tendency of a body to remain motionless or in motion without acceleration.

linear motion (LIN-ee-ur MOE-shun) Movement in a straight line.

mass (MASS) The measure of an object's inertia, the amount of matter that it contains, and its influence in a gravitation field.

momentum (moe-MEN-tum) The measure of movement; the resistance of an object to slowing down.

scalar (SKAY-lur) A quantity with magnitude but not direction.

speed (SPEED) A measure of how fast an object is moving with regard to time.

trajectory (tra-JEK-tuh-ree) The path a projectile makes through space.

vector (VEK-tur) A quantity with magnitude and direction.

velocity (va-LOS-uh-tee) The rate at which an object changes its position.

For More Information

American Center for Physics
One Physics Ellipse
College Park, MD 20740
(301) 209-3100
Web site: http://www.acp.org

NASA
300 E Street SW
Washington, DC 20546
(202) 358-0000
Web site: http://nasa.gov/home/index.html

National Science Foundation, Math and Physical Sciences
4201 Wilson Boulevard
Arlington, VA 22230
(703) 292-5111
Web site: http://www.nsf.gov/home/mps

Web Sites

Due to the changing nature of Internet links, the Rosen Publishing Group, Inc., has developed an online list of Web sites related to the subject of this book. This site is updated regularly. Please use this link to access the list:

http://www.rosenlinks.com/liph/lamo

For Further Reading

Adair, Robert K. *The Physics of Baseball*, 3rd ed. New York: Perennial, 2000.

Bloomfield. Louis A. *How Things Work: The Physics of Everyday Life.* New York: John Wiley & Sons, 1991.

Gardner, Robert. *Science Projects About the Physics of Sports.* Berkeley Heights, NJ: Enslow Publishing, 2000.

Hache, Allain. *The Physics of Hockey.* Baltimore: Johns Hopkins University Press, 2002.

Holthusen, Peter, and Art Arfons. *Fastest Men on Earth: 100 Years of the Land Speed Record.* Gloucestershire, England: Sutton Publishing, 2000.

Lopez, Carl, and Danny Sullivan. *Going Faster! Mastering the Art of Race Driving.* Cambridge, MA: Bentley Publishers, 2003.

McPherson, Joyce. *Ocean of Truth: The Story of Sir Isaac Newton.* Lebanon, TN: Greenleaf Press, 1997.

Bibliography

Bloomfield. Louis A. *How Things Work: The Physics of Everyday Life.* New York: John Wiley & Sons, 1991.

Elert, Glenn. *The Physics Hypertextbook.* Retrieved December 2003–March 2004 (http://www.hypertextbook.com/physics).

Henderson, Tom. *The Physics Classroom.* Retrieved March 2004 (http://www.physicsclassroom.com).

Stern D. R. *From Stargazers to Star Maps.* Retrieved January 2004 (http://www-spof.gsfc.nasa.gov/stargaze/ Sintro.htm#q3).

Tucek, Jim. *Interactive Physics.* Retrieved February 2004 (http://www.jracademy.com/~jtucek/physics/physics.html).

Index

A
acceleration, 10–11, 19, 21, 22, 23, 24, 30, 34, 35
applied force, 37, 41

B
ballistics, 19

C
centrifugal force, 16–17
centripetal force, 16–17
circular motion, 16–17
classical/Newtonian physics, explanation of, 4–5
conservation of momentum, 26–29

D
direction, 6, 7, 10, 11, 13, 14, 15, 20, 22, 23, 25, 27, 30, 36, 40, 41
displacement, 6, 7, 11, 12
distance, 6, 7, 10, 11, 12, 21, 31
dynamics, 13

E
electromagnetism, 31
equilibrium, 22, 37

F
forces, types of, 31–33
    applied force, 37, 41
    electromagnetism, 31
    friction, 10, 11, 18, 31, 35–36, 41, 42
    gravity, 10, 11, 13, 16, 18, 19, 20, 30, 31, 33–35, 37, 39, 41, 42

normal force, 37, 41, 42
    spring force, 37
    tension, 11, 31, 37–39, 41
free-body diagrams, 40–42
friction, 10, 11, 18, 31, 35–36, 41, 42

G
g force, 34–35
gravity, 10, 11, 13, 16, 18, 19, 20, 30, 31, 33–35, 37, 39, 41, 42

I
inertia, 21, 22, 25, 30, 31–33, 37

K
kinematics, 13, 14

L
linear motion, 15–16

M
magnitude, 6, 7, 10, 12, 22, 23, 25, 27, 37, 40, 41
mechanics, 13, 20
momentum, 22, 26–29
motion
    circular, 16–17
    dimensions of, 13–15
    explanation of, 6
    laws of, 4, 20–29, 30, 42
    linear, 15–16
    projectile, 19
    rotary, 17–18
    uniform, 9–10

N
Newton, Isaac, 20, 42
    first law of motion, 20–22, 30
    second law of motion, 23–25, 30
    third law of motion, 25–26, 30
newtons, 30–31
normal force, 37, 41, 42

P
projectile motion, 19

R
rotary motion, 17–18

S
scalar quantities, 7, 11, 39

speed, 4, 6, 7, 9, 10, 11, 16, 20
spring force, 37

T
tension, 11, 31, 37–39, 41
time, 7, 10, 11, 13

U
uniform motion, 9–10

V
vector diagram, 7
vector quantities, 7, 10, 11,
    22, 39
velocity, 6, 7, 10, 11, 19, 21, 22, 24,
    36, 41

About the Author

Betty Burnett lives in St. Louis, Missouri. She would like to acknowledge the help of John Freeman, Ph.D.; Lew Fowler; and Brad Rhomer in writing this book.

Photo Credits

Cover © Paul A. Souders/Corbis; p. 5 © Taxi/Getty Images; pp. 8, 12, 23, 26, 28, 41, 42 by Geri Fletcher; pp. 9, 33 courtesy of NASA; p. 15 © Louis K. Meisel Gallery/Corbis; p. 17 © Bettmann/Corbis; p. 18 © AP/Wide World Photos; p. 21 © David Woods/Corbis; p. 31 © Charles Walker/TopFoto/The Image Works; p. 32 © Bill Aron/Photo Researchers, Inc.; p. 35 © Stone/Getty Images; p. 38 © H&S Production/Corbis.

Designer: Tahara Anderson; **Editor:** Christine Poolos